T0198747

Maxx Curious

pt.#2 "He's at it again"

·······································

Joyce B. Whaley
"The Sunday School Teacher"

WestBow Press books may be ordered through booksellers or by contacting:

WestBow Press
A Division of Thomas Nelson & Zondervan
1663 Liberty Drive
Bloomington, IN 47403
www.westbowpress.com
1 (866) 928-1240

Because of the dynamic nature of the Internet, any web addresses or links contained in this book may have changed since publication and may no longer be valid. The views expressed in this work are solely those of the author and do not necessarily reflect the views of the publisher, and the publisher hereby disclaims any responsibility for them.

Any people depicted in stock imagery provided by Getty Images are models, and such images are being used for illustrative purposes only.
Certain stock imagery © Getty Images.

Scripture taken from the Amplified Bible, Copyright © 1954, 1958, 1962, 1964, 1965, 1987 by The Lockman Foundation. Used by permission.

ISBN: 978-1-9736-8321-6 (sc)
ISBN: 978-1-9736-8322-3 (e)

Library of Congress Control Number: 2020900337

Print information available on the last page.

WestBow Press rev. date: 1/30/2020

WestBow
PRESS®
A DIVISION OF THOMAS NELSON
& ZONDERVAN

Curious Maxx

pt.#2 "He's at it again"

Maxx is seven years old now and will be entering into the second grade. His mother Kyla recently got married and they all moved into a new house in a multicultural neighborhood. Both Kyla and her husband are bi-racial. Kyla is African American and Puerto Rican and Tudor her husband is Egyptian and Kenyan. Maxx's biological father is from Barcelona his father is fluent in Catalan and English. Maxx is fluent in Catalan and Spanish. It was a requirement that he learn the language of his heritage. Kyla and Tudor wanted to find a neighborhood that would embrace all ethnicities and that Maxx and their future children would be well rounded culturally.

The family moved into the new neighborhood the same week that the children were due back in school. So Maxx had not met or played with any of the children in the area. So school would be the first time that Maxx will see what his new neighborhood is comprised of.

The alarm went off in Kyla's room and she got out of bed and yelled rise and shine Maxx, your first day of school awaits. As she began to go down the hallway to his bedroom Maxx jumped out and said, "Surprise I am ready let's get it, let's go."

Kyla jumped backed a little from being surprised at him being up so early and then she said, "Oh my goodness buddy, did you get any sleep last night?" Maxx rubbing his eyes said, "Nope I will get some sleep tonight when this day is over." They both laughed out loud.

Maxx said, "Mom what if nobody likes me?"

Kyla stuttered and said, "W—h—a--t! Huh? Come again? Who could resist your smile, your personality or your cute little dimples? You are smart and very intelligent, and may I add very handsome. Do I need to say anymore?"

Maxx burst into laughter and says "Yeah mom I guess you are right." Then he put his head down on the table and said, "For real mommy what if nobody likes me."

Kyla said, "I am absolutely, positively sure that everybody in your class will like you. She said have I ever told you anything wrong?"

Maxx thought for a minute and said, "Yes mom a few times."

Kyla chuckled and said, "Okay, smarty pants, forget those few times. I am telling you that everybody is going to like you. So let me get showered and dressed so we can get this party started."

Kyla walks out of her room singing, "Lets –get--it started, let's -get -it -started, whoop! whoop!"

Maxx begins to think about all the changes that has happen in his little life so far and he says, Dear God I'm so scared". A new school, a new house, new neighborhood, new friends, new dad I'm scared. Mommy said that I can come to you about anything. So would you please make all the kids like me today, pretty please with sugar on top, Amen.

Kyla is dressed and begins to fix Maxx and Tudor breakfast. Maxx said, "Mommy I'm really not hungry this morning so don't fix anything for me."

Kyla said, "Wrong answer dude, you have to eat something. I don't care if it's a half of a banana or a small glass of orange juice. Maxx drinks the orange juice quickly and said, "Let's get this party started I'm tired and sleepy and nervous. I even think I feel diarrhea coming on."

Kyla said, "Oh my not diarrhea," they both chuckled.

Tudor enters the kitchen, Kyla, gives him a big kiss and whispers to him, "Maxx is having first day jitters."

Kyla said, Honey breakfast is in the microwave." Tudor shouts out as both Kyla and Maxx leaves out the house "break a leg Maxxo", Maxx mumbles under his breath, "Yeah thanks pops."

They both head towards the truck and Maxx goes to get into the front seat. Kyla says, "Ah excuse me buddy, what are doing? Please get in the back, in your car seat.

Maxx said, "Mommy please let me sit upfront with you. I will looked like a tall nerd crumped up in that car seat in the back. Plus sitting in the front would make me look cool.

Kyla said sternly, "Boy strap up in the back seat or we will walk four blocks to school, your choice." Maxx gets in his car seat in the back and keeps his window rolled up so that no one would see him.

Kyla pulls up to the school and they both jump out. Kyla grabs Maxx hand. Maxx pulls his hand back quickly and said, "Oooh Mommy what are you about to do, please do not hold my hand. I'm trying to make friends here." Kyla burst into laughter and said, "Boy what am I going to do with you."

Maxx said, "Mommy would you please pray that today be a good day. And please do not grab my hand, and… please pray quietly, please. Maxx said second grade is serious stuff you didn't know? Kyla said child you are putting too much pressure on me this early in the morning. Then she begins to laugh. Maxx said, "Mom please don't laugh I'm feeling a little sick right now."

Kyla said, "Oh my goodness this is serious, okay". She immediately whispers a prayer where only she and Maxx can hear. Kyla said, "Father God please bless Maxx's first day of school and the entire school year that it be filled with protection, friends, knowledge, quick understanding and excitement, in Jesus name we pray Amen." Maxx agrees by saying Amen.

Kyla walks Maxx to the front door of the building. Then she stops and watches him as proceeds to his class. She begins to cry a little and hurries up to wipe away her tears so that he cannot see them if he looks back at her. Once he enters the doorway he finds everybody already seated. As he enters his teacher Mrs. Harrington said, "And who are you?"

Maxx puts his head down and walks slowly to her and said, "My name is Maximilian Amir Whaley."

"Class would everyone please say hi to Maximilian Amir Whaley." The entire class shouts, "Hi Maxx!"

Maxx raised his head up in total surprise and laughs and said out loud, "How did you all know to call me Maxx?" The whole class burst out in laughter.

What Maxx does not know is that Kyla visited the school earlier during the week to meet Mrs. Harrington to share somethings about Maxx so that she could make him feel more at ease on his first day of school. Maxx sat down in the second row in between Vinnie and Chloe.

Vinnie is a very intelligent seven year old Italian and Greek lad. And Chloe is just as bright and pretty. Her family comes from Jaipur India.

Maxx settles into his new surroundings comfortably. And before you know it the bell sounds to dismiss the class for the day. Mrs. Harrington gave out homework assignments before the children ran out of class. Maxx runs out of the school with his new friends, Vinnie and Chloe. Maxx and Vinnie drop their book bags on the ground by a big willow tree and begin doing cartwheels. Chloe just walks a little behind them laughing at the both of them.

Kyla gets out of her truck and folds her arms and said, "My, my, my, it appears as if someone had a real good day."

Maxx said excitedly, "Mom, mom everybody liked me! And I mean everybody! And they all knew to call me Maxx. Today was G-R-E-A-T (this was said in Maxx's Tony the Tiger voice).

Maxx said, "I didn't get any sleep last night thinking nobody would like. I should have known that with my charm and personality and cute dimples everybody would like me. Both Kyla and Maxx burst out into laughter."

Kyla said, "Well Maxx, are you going to introduce me to your friends"?

Maxx said, "Oh, my bad, Mom this is Vinnie and Chloe, you all can call my mom Miss. K."

Kyla said, "Hi there. "Then she said, "Oh my goodness Chloe you have the prettiest eyes and Vinnie you have a strong hand shake."

Vinnie and Chloe both politely said, "Thank you Miss. K."

Vinnie and Chloe both see their parents and said their goodbye's to Maxx and they run off to meet them. Kyla immediately throws her hand up to wave at both of their parents.

As they begin to walk to the car Maxx says, "Mom I'm seven years old now and I think it time for me to begin calling you mom, instead of mommy is that okay?" Kyla said, "Sure, but she whispered to herself I knew that this day would come."

Maxx said, "I was talking in class and said Mommy and everybody laughed out loud and said, Whoa dude, nobody says Mommy anymore". The entire class fell out laughing at me. Kyla and Maxx both burst out into some series laughter. She said, "Quick comeback dude."

Kyla said, "Okay so tell me everything that happened in class."

Maxx said, "Well my teachers name is Mrs. Harrington and she always says things like fantabulous, fantastic, excellent or splendid or sorry wrong answer dude or missy. And I sit in between Vinnie, my new best friend and Chloe."

Maxx said, "Mom, Chloe is so fine!" Kyla said, "Huh, fine! What's that?"

Maxx said, "Mom her skin is like a Hersey's candy bar and her eyes are a real light like Uncle Marvin's eyes are." Kyla chuckled and said, "So, what does all that mean."

Maxx said, "She is not my girlfriend if that is what you are thinking. Vinnie told me that Chloe is his girlfriend. Kyla said, "Oh, so does that mean you can't like her?"

Maxx said, "Mom, Pops told me to get my grades right and learn all I can and the girls will come after me. He also said that I am a triple threat, plus Chloe is not crazy she will pick the right guy."

Maxx calls Kyla's husband Tudor, pops and his real father whose name is Sabastian, dad.

Kyla said, "Oh pops told you that huh? Maxx winked one of his eyes and said, me and pops talk about everything and I do mean everything, Mom. Kyla laughed and said I am picking up on everything you are putting down son. Maxx said I call it men talk.

Maxx said, Mom Chloe is always snapping her fingers and says bloop, after every sentence. She makes me think of you. Kyla said, "Oh, is that right, bloop"!

Kyla and Maxx get in the car and buckled their seat belts and begin driving. Maxx said, "Soooooo, once I got into class we stood to say the Pledge of Allegiance to the flag. Everybody stood up except Vinnie, Chloe and a few other kids. In my mind I said what was is really going on in this school. Should I bend down on one knee like the guy who plays football?

Kyla screamed in amazement, "Boy please stop, you are too funny." Maxx then says, "Mom, Vinnie told me that he is Muslim and that he doesn't say the pledge neither does not pray to Jesus, he prays to Allah, what is that all about? I thought that everybody prayed to Jesus! Then Chloe, she jumped in and said her family is Hindi or Hindu. What in the world is going on, can we all just come together and say the pledge and pray? Who doesn't pray to Jesus?"

Kyla screamed in laughter and said, "Boy please stop you are making my stomach hurt."

She then let out a great big sigh and said, "Woosau, he's at it again."

Maxx then said after we said the pledge of allegiance I was looking for Mrs. Harrington to say a quick prayer over the class. It was quiet as a church mouse as Nanny would say. Kyla said, "Maxx if you don't stop making me laugh I'm going to put you out of this truck". Mom would you please tell me why we do not pray in school? And can you explain why Vinnie and Chloe do not pray to Jesus? Because I was about to lay hands on them in Jesus name.

And can you please make it short because I have more to tell you more about my day?"

Kyla said, "Well Maxx, Christianity is not the only religion there is."

Maxx said, "Huh? What you talking about Lucy? (Lucy is a pet name that Maxx calls his mother when they are in joking mode).

"There are thousands of religions and Christianity is just one of them. And different religions require that you believe and do different things."

She then shakes her head and takes in a deep breath and whispers to herself, Lord please guide my mind and words so that I do not confuse Maxx on what he already believes oppose to what I am about to tell him. If Vinnie said that he is Muslim then he prays to Allah. That is another name that people call God and the messenger that they say Allah sent to speak to the people name is Muhammad. Maxx was about to say something when Kyla said, "Baby please do not interrupt me right now this is serious. And if Chloe said that she is Hindu then her religion believes in a God called Brahman. They believe that he is one Supreme Being and that he can show himself or be seen in many other things like plant life, animals and other elements to name a few."

Maxx then raised his hand as if he was in class and said. "Then how do people know if their God or what they believe is true?"

Kyla was sipping on her coffee when she spewed out a little on her lap and said, "Whoa dude. This is way too deep for 3:30 in the afternoon," she replied. "We will respect Vinnie and Chloe religions because our God gives everybody a right to choose. You are only seven years old and I do not want you to become confused with the different religions at this time so oppose to me telling you what Muslim's and Hindu's believe in detail I am about to breakdown to you what we believe as Christians. And if Vinnie and Chloe ever become curious about your faith then you stand your ground and share this with them.

Maxx said, "Mom is this going to take a long time because I have other things to tell you about my day."

Kyla replied, "Nope not at all. "We believe in an invisible God that lives in heaven and in our hearts at the same time. We believe that God moves in three characters however they all are in one body. Kyla slowed down for a moment and said do you understand me so far. Maxx said yes, it's something like me saying me, myself and I right? Kyla said exactly. She goes on to say, as far as I know in my research and studying the word of God, Christianity is the only religion where God lives on the inside of each person's heart that accepts Jesus as the Son of God. He can see and hear everything and everybody at one time. Therefore you can pray to him in your bedroom and I can pray to him while I am driving home from work and he listens to the both of us at the same time. So there is never a line waiting to get his attention."

"God enters into a person heart once they accept and believe that he sent his son, Jesus to die for every wrong that they did. Jesus preached about a place that we will go once we die called heaven. And we believe that Grandma Betty, Papa and Nanny are there. People crucified Jesus or another term killed him because he said that he was the Son of God. They also got very upset because he often talked about this invisible place in the sky called heaven."

Then a King named Pontus Pilate sentenced him to be beat and the soldiers later crucified him and nailed him to a tree where he eventually died from all the cruel punishment. They later placed him in a small cave and on the third day God raised him from the dead. So you ask me how Christians know that if God is true. Because you cannot see him but you can feel his presence often and you can see him through the various things he created like the stars, the moon and sun and that rainbow that appears in the sky after it rains."

"So every morning when we pray and every Wednesday or Sunday that we go to church, I am slowly introducing you into this belief system of Christianity. And we will trust in this Christian creed until we do not have any breathe in our bodies, do you understand that!" Maxx said jokingly, "Aye, Aye Captain."

Then Maxx said, "So Mom everybody doesn't run around church like Auntie Valerie thanking God for healing her when she was really, really sick?" Kyla replied, "Nope."

Maxx said, "So everybody doesn't shout in a corner like Auntie Tamara because he blessed her with a gazillion dollar paying job." Kyla replied, "Nope."

Maxx said, Okay mom one last question before I tell you about Chloe. How come we do not pray in school?"

Kyla said, "Grammy said years ago they used to pray in public school. But then a lady name Madalyn Murray O'Hair went to court to demand that prayer stopped being said. And after much research of the laws a Judge agreed with her and now prayer is no longer said."

Maxx said, "That includes Vinnie's and Chloe's religions." Kyla said, "Yes that includes both Vinnie and Chloe's religions."

Kyla then said, "That is why we get up early in the morning and pray to God before we leave out the house. If you can remember in our prayer time we solicit the aid of our Angels to keep us safe. As a matter of fact I'm positive that one of your bible verses that you have to remember for Sunday school says, "He will give His angels charge concerning you, to guard you in all your ways."

Kyla said, "Does not praying in school bother you?"

Maxx said, "Hmmm, not really, I am learning that God lives in two places at the same time. In my heart and nobody can take him out of there ever. And he sits on a big fat throne with all kinds of diamonds and jewels on it in heaven. And he can see everything and everybody at the same time, right?"

Kyla said, "You are absolutely, positively correct, give me a fist bump dude!" Kyla reaches her hand back and Maxx plays sleep. Kyla said, "Oh, second grade have you faking your mom out, huh?"

Maxx laughed out loud and said, "I was just kidding give me your old little fist."

Kyla said, "Nope I'm, good. I hope you know about payback. Both of them begin to laugh. All of a sudden the car got quiet and tears begin to roll down Kyla' face. She thought to herself that she had just witness to Maxx about the death, burial and resurrection of Jesus. Maxx said, Mommy are you okay up there"? Kyla replied, "yeah buddy I'm good, thanks for asking."

"Mom I have a question that I have been meaning to ask you but didn't know how to say it."

Kyla replied, "Well what is it buddy?" Maxx said, ah, ah, why didn't you marry my dad? Did I have anything to do with it?

Kyla coughed really loud and then cleared her throat even louder. She whispered under her breathe "Woosau would somebody please help me." They finally got to the house and pulled up into the driveway and she put the car in park. She said, "Maybe you should be a journalist instead or a neurologist."

Maxx said, "Wrong answer Lucy, pop's said, 'the moolah is understanding the brain'." She said, "I guess understanding the brain; it is," they both laughed out loud.

Kyla then said, "I'm going to make a long story child proof. Is there a particular reason why you asked that question?"

Maxx paused for a moment then he said, "Well Chloe, her mom, dad and little sister have the same last name. It is the same with Vinnie, his sister, mom and dad. You changed your name to Gamal after you married pops and now I am left alone with Whaley. What's up with that?"

Kyla said, "First of all you had nothing to do with your dad and I not getting married, point blank and the period." Maxx then gasped and said, "Ooh no, not the point blank and the period." That means nothing else to be said on that topic"?

Kyla said, A-to the men. Your dad and I both love you to the moon and back, you know that right?" Maxx said, "Yep."

Kyla then said, "You know how you and pops can sit up and watch Jurassic Park and the Ninja Turtles all night long?" Maxx said, "Yes."

"Well what if all of a sudden pops only wanted to watch Jurassic Park and not Ninja Turtles. Then after three weeks he doesn't want to watch Jurassic Park either, how would you feel?"

Maxx said, "Sad because that's what makes us come together and talk plus we eat tons and tons of pizza until my stomach hurts. I like that time because I don't have to share him with anybody in the whole wide world."

Well that's kind of what happened with your dad and me. His job kept him traveling all the time and all over the world. Eventually the things that we use to do, we didn't anymore so we slowly drifted apart do you understand that?" Maxx said, "I get it. I thought that it was something I did."

Kyla then said, when I gave birth to you I was not married to your dad. And Papa having old school ways strongly advise me to give you my last name and not Sebastian's so I obeyed my dad. Now you know the whole truth and nothing but the truth. She then said, "Does not having my new last name bother you? Maxx replied, "No, not since I understand why."

Maxx said, "hmm you see what happens when we talk about things?" Kyla laughed and said, "okay smarty pants. You sound like pops."

All of a sudden the phone rang and Kyla said hello through the radio speaker and Tudor said, "Hi honey I was calling to check up on my two favorite peeps in the whole wide world."

Maxx shouted out, "Hey pops today was G-R-E-A-T," in his Tony the Tiger voice. Tudor said, "That's cool I was praying for my little fella."

Maxx said, "Prayers answered again, ding! God did his thing again, ding! Can we sing Amen?" Tudor said, "Let the church sing A-m-e-n brother and sister Whaley. They all sang A-M-E-N and then burst into laughter.

Maxx said, "Hey pops, Tudor said, "What's up Maxxo?"

"Can we please watch the Ninja Turtles tonight?"

Tudor replied, "Hey buddy I was just about to ask you the same things."

Kyla said, "Can I join?

Tudor replied jokingly, "I think we have a bad connection on the phone. I love you honey, goodbye. See you at the man cave Maxxo."

The End!

Printed in the United States
By Bookmasters